Farm animals

Bobbie Kalman

Crabtree Publishing
crabtreebooks.com

Created by Bobbie Kalman

Author and Editor-in-Chief
Bobbie Kalman

Educational consultants
Elaine Hurst
Joan King
Jennifer King

Notes for adults
Jennifer King

Editors
Kathy Middleton
Crystal Sikkens

Design
Bobbie Kalman
Katherine Kantor

Print and production coordinator
Katherine Kantor

Prepress technician
Katherine Kantor

Photo research
Bobbie Kalman

Photographs
Photos.com: page 14 (top right)
Other photographs by Shutterstock

Crabtree Publishing

crabtreebooks.com 800-387-7650

Printed in Canada/072024/CPC20240725

Published in Canada
Crabtree Publishing
616 Welland Avenue
St. Catharines, Ontario
L2M 5V6

Published in the United States
Crabtree Publishing
347 Fifth Avenue
Suite 1402-145
New York, NY 10016

Hardcover 978-0-7787-9552-0
Paperback 978-0-7787-9577-3
Ebook (pdf) 978-1-4271-9659-0

Library and Archives Canada Cataloguing in Publication

Kalman, Bobbie, 1947-
Farm animals / Bobbie Kalman.

(My world)
Issued also in electronic format.
ISBN 978-0-7787-9552-0 (bound).--ISBN 978-0-7787-9577-3 (pbk.)

1. Domestic animals--Juvenile literature. 2. Livestock--Juvenile literature. I. Title. II. Series: My world (St. Catharines, Ont.)

SF75.5.K34 2011 j636 C2010-907427-0

Library of Congress Cataloging-in-Publication Data

Kalman, Bobbie.
Farm animals / Bobbie Kalman.
p. cm. -- (My world)
ISBN 978-0-7787-9577-3 (pbk. : alk. paper) -- ISBN 978-0-7787-9552-0 (reinforced library binding : alk. paper) -- ISBN 978-1-4271-9659-0 (electronic (pdf))
1. Livestock--Juvenile literature. I. Title.
SF75.5.K35 2011
636--dc22

2010047120

Words to know

Some animals live on farms.
This boy is feeding
some farm animals.
He helps take care of them.

These girls live on a farm, too.
They help take care of the lambs.

These are some farm animals with their babies. What are their names?

chicken

chick

horse

foal

duckling

duck

sheep
pig
piglet
lamb
cow
goat
calf
kid

Many horses live on farms.
People like to ride horses.
This girl is riding a horse.

A foal is a baby horse.
This foal is drinking
its mother's milk.
A foal eats grass, too.

A lamb is a baby sheep.
This lamb is drinking milk.
A lamb eats grass, too.

Lambs and sheep have **wool** coats. The wool is used to make clothes for you and me.

The wool is cut off.

This boy's hat and scarf are made from wool.

Cows, goats, and chickens
give us food to eat.
We get eggs from chickens.

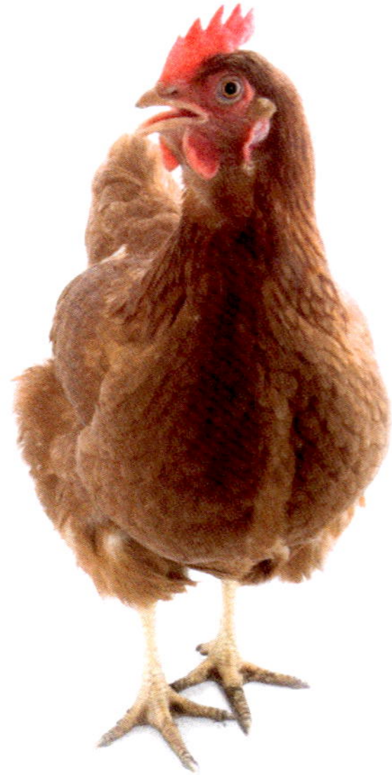

chicken

eggs

cow

goat

We get milk from cows and goats. Cheese and butter are made from milk.

cheese

milk

butter

Talk like an animal!

Which animal talks like this?

1. moo
2. oink
3. baaa
4. quack
5. neigh

Answers

1. cow 2. piglet 3. lamb
4. duckling 5. horse

Can you touch your nose the way this cow can?
This cow says
“noo”!

Notes for adults

Objectives

- to identify farm animals and their babies
- to explore with children the products animals give us
- to have children appreciate the resources we get from animals

Before reading book

Write these frequently used words on the board:
a, an, are, baby, boy, can, care, eat, food, from, get, give, hat, have, he, help, in, is, it, its, like, live, many, of, on, says, some, take, the, them, these, they, this, to, too, us, we, what, with, you, your

Ask these questions:
"What foods do you eat for breakfast?"
"Where does the milk for your cereal come from?"
"Where do we get our eggs from?" "Where do butter and cheese come from?"

Bring in some packaging from animal products: milk carton, egg container, or butter and cheese packaging. Have the children guess which products were in the packages and where they came from.

Questions after reading book

"What can children do on a farm?"
(go horseback riding, help feed the animals)
"List the foods you eat from different animals."
(cow–milk, goat–cheese, chicken–eggs)
"What do sheep give us to keep us warm?" (wool)

Ask children to match these adult animals with their babies:
A chicken has a ... (chick).
A horse has a ... (foal).
A duck has a ... (duckling).
A sheep has a ... (lamb).
A cow has a ... (calf).
A pig has a ... (piglet).

Activity: Sound and sing

Ask each child to make an animal sound, such as one of the sounds on page 14. Ask the other children to guess which animal made that sound. Ask the children to sing "Old MacDonald had a Farm" using the animals and the sounds in the book. Then challenge them to try to touch their noses with their tongues. "Who can do what the cow on page 15 can do?"

Extension

Ask the children to write thank-you cards to the animals whose products they enjoy. They can draw pictures of themselves using the products.

For teacher's guide, go to www.crabtreebooks.com/teachersguides